# Old Carradale

## Iain Wright

CW00558194

The war memorial on the right of this photograph was erected by public subscription next to the Mitchells' house at the east end of Airds in September 1920, to commemorate the fourteen local men who died in World War I and subsequently the two who died in World War II. Its location was chosen because the Mitchell family had lost two sons in the war. It is made of granite, similar to the Cenotaph in Glasgow's George Square. A popular diversion for the men of Carradale was indulging in games of pitch and toss at the war memorial. Pennies were aimed with great enthusiasm at an upright stick and the player whose coin landed closest lifted the accumulated pile, after a heads or tails playoff. There was a drinking fountain close to the memorial which provided fresh water to the residents. A government scheme was completed in 1956, enabling indoor tap supply from tanks above Moineruadh and Airds which were fed by two streams flowing high into Carra Water above the village. The supply was beset with problems though, especially during dry summer months, and sometimes resulted in a brackish brown tap delivery. Carradale Hotel is behind the wall on the left; the sign advertises the petrol it supplied and the barrels and boxes presumably also belong to it. Further down on the left-hand side is Paterson's Bakery with Ashbank Hotel in the distance.

Text © Iain Wright, 2020.
First published in the United Kingdom, 2020,
by Stenlake Publishing Ltd.,
54-58 Mill Square,
Catrine, Ayrshire,
KA5 6RD

Telephone: 01290 551122
www.stenlake.co.uk

Printed by Blissetts, Unit 1, Shield Drive,
West Cross Industrial Park, Brentford, TW8 9EX

ISBN 9781840338942

**The publishers regret that they cannot supply copies of any pictures featured in this book.**

## Acknowledgements

My grateful thanks and appreciation for their helpful advice and extensive information are due in particular to Angus Martin and Christine Ritchie.

In addition my thanks are due to Maureen Bell, Sharon Bell, Ronnie Brownie, Colin Burgess, Pam Galbraith, Freddy Gillies, Niall Macalister-Hall, John Martin, John McFadyen, Argyll McMillan, Alisdair Paterson, Archie Paterson, Lachie Paterson, William Paterson, Dominic Ryan, Robert Strang, Alan Walker, David Walker and especially my ever patient wife and 'adopted local' Helen for her support throughout. Thanks also to David Pettigrew for his editing skills.

The author and publishers wish to thank the following for contributing photographs to this book: Johnny Durnan (pages 12 (both), 14, 15, 16, 22, 25, 26, 53 (both) and 56); Cara Erskine (pages 23 and 24); John Martin (page 35); Nonnie MacAlister (page 50); National Library of Scotland (pages 36 and 52 (both)); Edna Paterson (page 28); and Mary Paterson (pages 13, 27 and 54).

*This book is dedicated to Archie Paterson, doyen of herring fishermen, with whom I spent many happy days and nights on the* Harvest Queen.

## Further Reading

The books listed below were used by the author during his research. None is available from Stenlake Publishing. Those interested in finding out more are advised to contact their local bookshop or reference library.

Burgess, M., (ed), *NM Essays and Journalism Volume 2 Carradale,* Zeticula, 2009
Gillies, F., *The Viking Isle*, Ardminish Press, 2003
Martin, A., *Fish and Fisherfolk of Kintyre*, House of Lochar, 2004
Martin, A., *Herring Fishermen of Kintyre*, House of Lochar, 2002
Martin, A., *The Ring-Net Fishermen*, John Donald Publishers Ltd, 1981
McIlvride, E., *Rauch the Wind*, private publication, Glasgow, 2017
Rixson, D. & M., *Carradale: Historical Guide from Saddell to Sunadale,* 1983
Robins, N.S., & Meek, D.E., *The Kingdom of MacBrayne*, Birlinn, 2008
Smyllie, M., *Herring: A History of the Silver Darlings*, Tempus Publishing Ltd, 2004
Walker, A.G.T., *Carradale Golf Club*, Brandfire, 2017

# Introduction

Carradale lies on the east side of the peninsula of Kintyre. Its nearest neighbour 14 miles south is Campbeltown, while Lochgilphead is 38 miles to the north. It is said that no-one ends up in Carradale who hasn't actually set out to be there, as the B842 bypasses the main part of the village.

There are signs of ancient settlement in the area. In Carradale Glen is a three-metre-high standing stone, known as the 'Toothie Stane', which superstition suggests cures toothache if a person suffering from it drives a nail into the stone at midnight. There are some 29 such marks on the stone. On the summit of Carradale Point, with a situation commanding the Kilbrannan Sound to the north and south, stands the ruins of an Iron Age vitrified fort. The Vikings arrived from about 800 AD, leaving their names as Sunadale, Carradale and Torrisdale (dale or *dalr* is Norse for 'valley'). The land was owned by Campbells since 1700, then granted to lairds in Carradale and Torrisdale who paid feu duty to the Duke of Argyll, earned from rents paid by their tenants. The first *Statistical Account* records the population of the parish of Saddell and Skipness as 1,341 in 1792, of whom 389 were aged under 10. The number peaked at 2,191 in 1821, falling to 1,798 by 1841, due partly to emigration to America. There used to be a road over the hills from Tayinloan to Auchenbreck and down to Carradale, and there was a village halfway across – Narachan. Now only the shells of its houses remain.

Carradale has been a fishing village for hundreds of years. Boats from there and other Clyde ports fished in Loch Fyne for herring in the sixteenth century. Sixty-five herring boats operated out of Saddell and Skipness parish in 1837; these had been going to the Minches in the spring using the Crinan Canal from 1801. The local fishermen were collectively known as 'the Crofters' or 'the Caardlemen'. Their accent is more of a Highland sing-song tongue peppered with Gaelic derivations and is unique to the village. An article in the *Economist* magazine in 2013 records that 'Fishing was more than an occupation in the village. The community was founded on it. Youths went to sea in their uncle's boats, formed ring-netting pairs with their neighbours, married one another's sisters and celebrated by drinking and singing songs about herring. These happy traditions are no more. Few sing about herring these days. Nobody sings about prawns.'

Smuggling of tea, wines and tobacco was widespread throughout Kintyre, as was the illicit distillation of whisky, to which the Church paid a blind eye. Smuggling was the main employment of crofters and fishermen in winter and Grogport, five miles north of Carradale, was the embarkation point for illicit distillers on west Kintyre; however, by the 1840s smuggling had been almost entirely suppressed.

Throughout the twentieth century fishing, tourism and agriculture remained the mainstays of the local economy. The village hall became a centre of social activity for Carradale. Many a romance blossomed at dances held there and lifelong friendships were forged with the visitors. Films were shown regularly. There were no streetlights in Carradale until 1960 so the long trek to and from the hall was quite an adventure. Naomi Mitchison, the laird for many years, maintained and upgraded the hall and generally took an active part in community life. For over a century the golf course has been one of the major attractions of the village. The heyday of holiday golfers lasted from the 1950s to the 1970s, when visitors queued in the mornings to book a place using the green ball board before returning after breakfast to play.

By 2009 the population was 1,350 and the area continues to have great natural attraction. From the heights of Dippen Brae in early summer, the first breathtaking glimpse of Carradale West and its lovely fertile glen is one which is bounded by a frame of tall, dark green coniferous trees and wild rhododendron bushes resplendent in their blazing natural colours. Of seventeen streams that run to Kilbrannan Sound much the largest is Carra Water, which has salmon and trout fishing. The Glen enjoys a great degree of heat and fertilising showers, which are highly favourable to agriculture. Valuable farming is practised in the Glen at Rhonadale and Lag Kilmichael. The Forestry Commission has covered the area with large scale afforestation following its acquisition of 13,000 acres from Carradale estate in 1937, when it promised not to encroach on good agricultural land, but to use rough hill land.

One of Carradale's oldest residents, currently in his seventies, was raised in the southernmost of the Airds cottages and still lives there. His father, a worker on Carradale estate, bought the house in 1946 after previously being a tenant and achieved a discount of £20 off the purchase price because the house had a gable end and would require more heating. The elder son of the family was a herring fisherman until the 1970s, when he opened a kippering business on the Shore Road, where there were two similar businesses. The current resident of the cottage was himself a very successful clam fisherman. The large tree outside the hotel was removed in order to improve parking facilities.

Airds has been the centre of Carradale for many years, with a shop, post office, hotel and golf course all within walking distance. Low Airds cottages on the immediate right-hand side have front doors at the back, as the laird, Austin Mackenzie, did not want to see washing hanging next to the main street. Airds' name comes from Gaelic for a height or promontory. Behind Airds cottages, at the top of a steep embankment lies the entrance to the Airds wood where local children love to play. Beyond Airds on the right is Bayview, built in the early twentieth century initially as a private house and then made available for the expanding tourist trade. Its owner was Walter Paterson – known as Wal – who retired to the extensive back house during the summer. He was a well-read man known for his sagacity and also for his poetry, which he wrote as the 'Carradale Bard'. Further down on the left side is Ashbank, which served as a post office for a number of years.

A busy retail outlet at Airds was Paterson's Bakery, which combined baking, grocery, butcher and dairy interests. Its morning rolls, bread and cookies were famed far and wide and the smell of freshly baked rolls in the early morning was an attraction in itself. People from Campbeltown were known to drive the sixteen miles to the shop for a supply. Another exalted product of the Patersons – particularly popular at New Year – were huge steak pies cooked in the bakehouse ovens. The shop sold newspapers and acted as a social meeting point for the entire village. In the early days deliveries were made by horse and cart. Subsequently they also operated a mobile shop for the local community, both of which methods offered current gossip to the local customers. In recent years the business suffered from supermarket competition in Campbeltown.

The bakery was founded by Archibald Paterson between 1861 and 1865 in Airds Cottage which was across the road from this building (it moved here between 1867 and 1874). The business was then owned in succession by John, George, John (with Dodie) and ended with John's daughter who maintained the operation until 2016 and the building is now empty. Outside the shop was a bus stop for the thrice-daily service to Campbeltown from 1936 (now five times daily) and the thrice-weekly service north to Tarbert on the east coast B842 which ended in the 1970s. A regular trip operated by West Coast Motors to Campbeltown was made on Monday mornings in the summer during the 1950s and 60s, with three buses often required to accommodate all the visitors and fishermen, who then sailed back in the herring boats to Carradale in time for lunch: the boats had been moored in the harbour over the weekend.

Passengers waiting for a steamer at the old pier, *c.* 1910. The first pier master was John Ritchie (1816-1888), followed in the Pier House by his son, also named John (1853-1933) and the great-grandfather of a current village resident. The Pier House, which can be seen on the far right of this photograph, was constructed in 1859 and has remained occupied since then. One of the pier master's jobs was to issue gale warnings to passing ships; for this a cone-shaped bag was hoisted on a tall mast on the hill beside the house and this pointed upwards for northerly gales and downwards for southerlies. There was also a mercury-filled barometer in the pier's waiting-room which had to be reset daily to warn of any impending storms. The Pier House was sold to local man David Oman by William Mackenzie, nephew of the previous laird, Austin Mackenzie, in September 1938.

The steamers *Davaar* and *Kinloch*, of the Campbeltown and Glasgow Steam Packet Joint Stock Company and sailing between those two locations, provided the main link between Kintyre and the outside world. *Davaar*, seen here around 1925, was built in 1885 to take the place of the *Gael*, a paddle steamer which had an impressive top speed of sixteen knots. *Davaar* had a classic clipper bow and figurehead. She ran aground in Belfast Lough in 1895, but was pulled to safety two days later, and was reboilered in 1903 with only one funnel. She was taken out of service as a steamer on the Kintyre Coast in 1939 and during World War II was intended to become a blockship at Newhaven in Sussex. However, she was eventually broken up on the beach in 1943 at the age of 58, her parts being of more use to the war effort than leaving her intact.

Herring were originally landed by boat on the beach at Carradale Bay. However, in 1857 the laird of Carradale estate, Sir David Carrick Robert Carrick Buchanan of Drumpellier, erected a wooden landing pier in the hope that the steamers of the Campbeltown Steam Packet Company, the *Druid* and *Celt,* would call on their passage four days weekly to and from Glasgow. It turned out to be a suitable landing place only when weather permitted, with the result that passengers were occasionally stranded in Carradale. The *Greenock Telegraph* of 23 August 1870 reported that 'a massive new iron pier is in course of erection at Carradale, which will enable steamers to come alongside in any state of the weather'. This pier was made of cast-iron which offered greater durability than wood and was the first of its kind in Scotland; it cost £4,000 and was financed entirely by the laird. It was designed on two levels (which can be seen more clearly in the next photograph), with a ramp between them to facilitate the fishing fleet as well as the regular passenger and cargo traffic, and it secured a regular steamer call which led to the development of tourism to the area.

*Kinloch*, seen here, was delivered as a sister ship to *Kintyre* in 1878 to deal with the developing summer excursion traffic. One of the most beautiful Clyde steamers, she was built as the first screw steamer for the Campbeltown & Glasgow Steam Packet Joint Stock Company's fleet. *Kinloch* was replaced by the *Dalriada* in 1926, the fastest single screw vessel in the United Kingdom. Licensed to carry 1,294 excursionists, she reduced the passage time between Gourock and Campbeltown to three hours and allowed the opportunity for charter trips in the early season to places such as Carradale. The direct steamer service from Campbeltown to Glasgow, calling at Carradale, was discontinued at the outbreak of World War II and never reinstated. *Dalriada* was sunk by a mine in 1942 while acting as a mercantile auxiliary in the Thames.

The fishermen had been asking for a harbour to replace the cast-iron pier for three generations and plans were frequently suggested, including a scheme in 1930 which had an estimated cost of £30,000 and had substantial support from the fishermen. But scheme after scheme was put forward and then discarded. Through a combination of government finance and local fundraising the new harbour finally took shape at a cost of £61,000 in 1959, under the benevolent eye of Tom Johnston, the highly regarded Secretary of State for Scotland, who had lobbied the case throughout the 1950s.

The old pier's iron hooped structure offered limited protection from northerly and easterly winds and by the 1950s its wooden surface was rotting away, although the resultant holes allowed youngsters to dangle fishing lines below in the hope of catching saithe. The new walled pier's surface is concrete and it is formed of thick interlocking sheet steel pilings, with steel cross bracings between the inner and outer sides, and large stone rubble in between the two sets of pilings. It was lit with a flashing beacon at the same time as most of the village was given street lighting. A newsagent and confectionery shop had stood at the entrance to the old pier, but it was demolished after the new pier was built. On opening day, 17 September 1959, the fishing fleet and the crane were decorated with coloured bunting.

Built in 1946 for its maiden voyage on the Firth of Clyde the following year, the *Waverley* is the last sea-going passenger-carrying paddle steamer and replaced her namesake, which was lost in the evacuation from Dunkirk in 1940. She sailed annually after World War II in Scotland and the south of England but was withdrawn from service in 1974. She was converted from coal to diesel fuel in 1957 and was described as a vessel of pre-eminent national significance. She was sold to the Paddle Steamer Preservation Society for £1 in 1974 and since then she has operated successfully as a charity, entertaining over six million passengers and following similar routes as before. She is based at Craigendoran on the Clyde, where low water allows safe berthing. Her regular cruise destinations include Dunoon, Rothesay, Largs, Tarbert, Brodick and Campbeltown, but she made one unique call on a foggy day at Carradale on 27 April 1992. Visitors were allowed on board for one hour to inspect the ship.

A snapshot of a family holiday at Torrisdale Bay, 1939. During the summer months in the busy tourist season it was commonplace to spend the afternoons at one of the beaches close to Carradale and the pier. Torrisdale Bay was the furthest south of these and its stony beach is close to the main road, although it suffered from biting clegs. South Dippen was steeply shelving and also stony, but it had a large grassed area behind the beach where families could play games and where Scouts camped for many years. The mile-long shallow Silver Sands allowed visitors and locals to enjoy the sand dunes for relaxation, playing games and swimming. After she came into service in 1947, during the afternoons the strong wash from the Campbeltown steamer *Duchess of Hamilton* rolled ashore; she was retired in 1970.

*Dalriada* would call at both Carradale and Pirnmill on the Isle of Arran. She is seen here leaving Carradale in 1938.

*Davaar,* seen here, sailed from Campbeltown for the Clyde on alternate days to *Dalriada,* with calls at Carradale, Lochranza, Gourock and Greenock. Since one was always on the homeward trip as the other was outward bound, their schedule allowed the day-tripper a few hours either in Glasgow from Campbeltown, or vice-versa. Brief stops were made at the intermediate ports.

Carradale, May 1929. 'No herring, no wedding' is a familiar saying among many fishing communities. In Tarbert, Loch Fyne, in 1871 the herring catches were miserable and there were no weddings there or in Lochgilphead that year. Drift-net fishermen were strongly against ring-netters on the grounds that they destroyed the herring spawn and fry, broke up the herring shoals and scared them away. However, earnings were much higher from ring-netting. An Act of Parliament in 1851 made ring-netting illegal, but it proved unenforceable and was repealed in 1867. 'Trawl' netters offloaded catches to steamers in the Clyde which took them to railheads at Ardrossan and Fairlie for onward transportation to Glasgow, beating the drift netters to market. Nets were made of hemp twine, then cotton from 1860. Much effort was expended by the fishermen to preserve their nets from rapid decay. Cutch, from acacia trees native to India, was bought in and dissolved in boiling water, in which the nets were steeped, a process also known as 'barking'. Damaged nets would be repaired on board using needles carved from bone, elder or other woods; more significant tears were repaired on shore.

Another view from May 1929. Nets were draped over poles with triple uprights lashed to a central trunk, to allow for natural drying, mostly at weekends. Cotton nets tended to become hot and would have coarse salt applied to prevent this. The quay brae up from the harbour passes on the left Portcrannag, which was built as a shop, and then the houses Duncrannag and Ardcraig, both of which were built for locals and then made available to cater for the burgeoning tourist trade from the mid-nineteenth century. As time passed, some of the more well-heeled visitors bought land and built permanent holiday homes above the Shore Road and in the Broomfield and Hill 60 areas which enabled them to spend winter weekends and breaks there (Hill 60 was named after a battlefield location at Ypres due to the blasting of rock for house building in the 1920s). The interesting designs of the new dwellings enhanced Carradale's housing landscape. The beach at Portcrannag was used to create a concrete slip in the 1960s which allowed for the unloading of heavy electrical equipment before its transport by road to the sub-station at the far end of the village. The Bungalow Tearoom (see page 30) can be seen above the shore in the centre of the photograph.

Ring-netters at Waterfoot. Depending on wind direction, Port Righ Bay, Carradale Bay and Waterfoot provided safe shelter for the fishing fleet. Waterfoot allowed the boats to sail up the Carra Water and benefit from maintenance to their hulls, including removal of barnacles and then painting. However, two factors alone altered the face of fishing in the period after the 1980s. Firstly, engine power increased dramatically and secondly, electronic technology led to a much more effective means of finding the fish. The most advanced ring-netters like those seen here, the last of which were built in the sixties and early seventies, were between 50 and 63 feet long, wooden built, each with a cruiser stern and a large wheelhouse. Ring-netting had been the most efficient method of herring fishing in the world but the advent of pair-trawling by powerful boats towing huge nets meant that the ringers just could not compete and tradition had again to make way for the march of progress. The last ring-netter fished in 1990. The fishing had lasted around 120 years, but its decline was irreversible.

The hamlet of Waterfoot was often used for mooring boats in winter, as the old Carradale pier did not provide an all-weather harbour for fishing boats. Between the wars seine-netting for white fish and dredging for scallops were introduced to the Clyde. At first these methods were employed only when herring fishing was slack but ultimately, in the post-war period, there were those who specialised and completely abandoned herring fishing. When the market for prawns expanded in the late 1950s, even more herring fishermen switched to prawn trawling, first as a seasonal job and finally as virtually an all-year-round occupation. By the 1960s ring-netting was therefore pursued only by the most committed of crews. Finally, in the early 1970s, the ring-net was entirely abandoned and trawls alone used.

The River Carra with Carradale House in the background. It took many years for Scottish ring-net fishing to evolve. In Loch Fyne in the 1830s drift nets were tied together and used to encircle herring shoals. Small open sailing boats called skiffs were widely used, but from the 1880s Loch Fyne skiffs were adapted with half-decking forward. In 1905 there were 36 skiffs based in Carradale. The first Carradale-based Loch Fyne skiff was the *Lady Carrick Buchanan* in 1907 and later that year Campbeltown fisherman Robert Robertson added an engine to his boat *Brothers*, the first in a west coast fishing boat. Soon after, he installed an engine into each of two modern decked netting boats named *Falcon* and *Frigate-Bird* in 1921, which both had longer hulls, canoe sterns, small wheelhouses, better accommodation, full decking and shortened sails. As engines became more reliable, dependence on sails was reduced and thus evolved what was termed the motor 'ringer', powered by an engine rather than sails. Fishing was an altogether family affair and son followed father into the job. This produced a sense of belonging in fishing communities, and a tradition not to be broken.

The *Westering Home* crew included George MacMillan and Donald McConnachie seen here with an unidentified fisherman on the right. Dinner on board was primarily herring and mountains of potatoes. A pot of soup would be sitting on the cooker and the kettle was always on the boil. The men on deck were often drenched by flying spray, even when wrapped up in protective clothing. The romantic image of a fisherman in glistening oilskins actually meant that he was soaked to the skin with condensation inside the garments. Average wage was £30 per man per week in 1953. Fishing boat shares of gross income less expenses were divided 50% to the skipper for maintenance of boat and gear and 50% for four crew. Fishermen were superstitious about the word 'salmon', for which substitutes such as 'billy', 'red fish' or 'queer fellow' were used. They also did not welcome on board a minister. Boats worked in pairs and the *Westering Home's* 'neighbour' boat was *Elma*.

*Opposite*: Boats were crewed by five men and a boy, who had the hardest task of hauling the hard surface rope (backrope) to which the corks were attached. Hauling was the hardest work and before winches were introduced this was all done by hand with the men from both boats standing in a row pulling. As the net came over the side of the boat the herring were brailed on board by a butterfly net. Some had to be removed by hand. The net remained on deck and, after a catch had been stowed in the hold, was hauled aft on to the port quarter in readiness for shooting again. With hours spent on a pitching deck covered in fish slime, often in cold and wet conditions, hands with no gloves being torn by netting and stung by jellyfish (known as "scowders"), and muscles aching, the work was exceptionally hard. Fishing could also be dangerous: the Carradale skiff *Mhairi* (CN 130) was lost during a squall off the coast at Bunlarie on 8 March 1911, causing the deaths by drowning of Walter McIntosh, his sons Dugald and Walter and his nephew John. A plaque was erected at Carradale pier in 2011 to commemorate this sad event. The men shown in this 1959 photograph are John Ramsay, Donald McConachie, Ronnie Brownie, Bill McMillan and Donald McAllister.

The crew of the *Florentine* were *(left to right)*: Donald MacAllister, Bill McMillan and brothers Walter (reclining above), John and James McConnachie. There was also their cousin Donald McConnachie, not present when the photograph was taken. Their neighbour boat was *Bairn's Pride*. The ring-net fishermen relied on signs from natural phenomena to find shoals. The sight of a gannet in daylight diving from high and plummeting into the sea was a sure sign of herring lurking below. Seagulls feeding on the surface and dark patches of water also signified the presence of herring. At night the phosphorescence of fish near the surface became visible by the boat's passage. Thumping the top rail with a hammer disturbed the herring by the sound waves created, which could show their presence. Another method involved a long length of piano wire, the end of which held a lead weight, which was towed slowly through the water. Experienced hands could tell when the wire came into contact with herring, rather than other fish.

Basking sharks are also found in local waters. In September 1937 a small sailing boat was fishing for mackerel when a breaching shark capsized their boat, drowning two adults and one child. An aggregation of 26 basking sharks was spotted off the pier one day in the 1960s. One of the unlikeliest commercial fishing ventures ever to have been established in Kintyre, and recorded in these photographs, was a basking shark processing station set up in 1938 by a young Englishman, Tony Watkins, seen here on the left with John Paterson (see next page) beside the mast. He fitted out an ex-herring boat, the *Dusky Maid*, with a

Norwegian-made harpoon and a Carradale crew, with several more men on shore to operate the liver boilers. The shark oil was used for Tilley lamps in the fishing boats. The 1939 Clyde season was a success, but Watkins was called up for military service in World War II. A Carradale man, John Paterson, covered in his absence with herring-fishing, and on his return after the war, the catching fleet was extended up to three, resulting in several successful shark-fishing summer seasons. Watkins wrote a book entitled *The Sea, My Hunting Ground*, in which he wrote 'how lucky he was to have taken on John Paterson'.

The shark carcasses were discarded in the sea and caused an unpleasant smell for the locals. The venture ended in the early 1950s and the concrete remains of the slipway and factory building, along with rust-bound machinery components, can still be seen at the Black Port, past the end of the Shore Road. A similar shark processing plant was set up in the mid 1940s on Soay, off Skye, by residents Tex Geddes and the author Gavin Maxwell, but it only lasted three years.

There were three dairy farmers who doubled as milk roundsmen: Duncan Semple of Dippen, who bought his ground in 1938, John MacKinnon of Auchnasavil, and Colin and Dodie Paterson of Airds, whose family home Kilbrannan villa, seen here, was built in 1887. Their cows left their visiting cards twice daily on the road between the milking parlour and their field. Initially the milk was poured from churns into people's jugs, then bottles of milk were delivered by hand via a milkboy on foot or by horse and cart to boarding houses and private dwellings. There was also a second delivery in late afternoons. Milking machines, which arrived in the late 1920s, and the advent of compulsory pasteurisation and regulations on minimum herd size, brought an unwelcome end to these activities, with the loss of high-protein warm milk straight from the cow. Milk subsequently arrived from Campbeltown.

Lochpark Stores in the centre of this view was founded by Peter McKinven and his wife Ellen Galbraith and subsequently run by Ellen's nephew, Dick Galbraith, originally a fisherman, and his wife Mary. In addition to the usual groceries and clothes and footwear, they also offered children famous knickerbocker glory and banana split ice creams. The shop even had a television and a jukebox and served tea and coffee, making it the place to recuperate after a morning's round of golf. Adjacent lay the Lochpark boarding house, run by two sisters, with six non-ensuite bedrooms. All meals were included, but residents had to be on hand sharp for breakfast at 9 a.m., lunch at 1 p.m. and high tea from 5.30 p.m. As was the custom for villagers letting out their houses, the ladies retired for the summer months to an extensive back house.

Further down Quay Brae was the Bungalow Tearoom and confectioner's shop, run from the late 1920s by Duncan Ritchie and Amy Harris until their son John took over with daughter-in-law Chattie. They sold coffee and first-class ice cream drinks and the tearoom also offered a beautiful view over the harbour as well as a television for customers. Some time after her husband passed away, Chattie emigrated to New Zealand to be with family. For a time a branch of the Bank of Scotland operated in the building one day a week, on a similar basis to the Royal Bank branch further up the brae. In turn, Chattie's daughter and son-in-law took possession of the tearoom, demolished it, and built a private house on the site.

Duncrannag was one of several large houses built by prosperous fishermen and which later catered for the growing number of tourists coming to the village during the inter-war period. The ground was feud by Austin MacKenzie in 1923 and the property lies adjacent to Ardcraig and Drumfearne and opposite Craigmore and Kenmore, houses which also became tourist summer homes. About £30 a month would be realised between the wars, with similar rates charged by boarding houses in Port Righ including Dunvalanree, Dunolly and Dunalastair. For decades, tourists came to Carradale for up to four weeks every year until the 1970s, when the allure of foreign holidays in guaranteed sunshine began to take its toll. The back houses, to which the locals retired, were substantial affairs, made of corrugated iron and wood. A famous suffragette, Flora Drummond, had spent her childhood in Pirnmill on Arran and in Carradale, and after she retired in 1944 she lived in this house until her death in 1949 and was buried in Brackley cemetery.

During the inter-war years a number of single-storey bungalows were built on open farm ground to the east of the centre of the village, in an area known as Lochpark. Between 1928 and 1932, provision for water and sewerage services was made to the area and the layout for these future streets was included. Quarter-acre plots for construction were conveyed by the landowners Duncan Semple and the Paterson family between 1950 and 1970. Towards the end of World War II Argyll Council proposed the building of fifty houses in the village, later reduced to forty, and these were built around the Port Righ crossroads. These prefabricated buildings were required to have a minimum floor space of 635 square feet and a maximum width of 7.5 feet, a size that allowed them to be transported by road to the site. They were constructed around a central service unit, which comprised a kitchen and bathroom prebuilt in a factory. Residents were encouraged to plant gardens. The houses were designed with a lifespan of 15 to 20 years, but many were lived in far longer than that, the last one remaining until the early 1960s. One was later moved from its site to provide office accommodation at the back of the Carradale Hotel.

Close to the Carradale Hotel were the bowling green and tennis court (the former seen here on the left with the latter behind the house in the centre), but these fell into disuse before 1939 and have since been built on for housing. One of Carradale's oldest current residents remembers playing as a child on the red blaize court. Another recalls a visitor challenging one of the locals to a bowling match on regular occasions, which caused him to lose his customary £1 bet on the outcome! Further to the west, located in front of Kilbrannan Villa was a large field, now built over, which was flooded during cold winters and provided an outdoor ice skating rink.

The first post office in Carradale was at Bridgend: in 1843 Duncan McCallum, a grocer of Carradale Bridge, was appointed as 'Receiver, Carradale' by the British Postal Service. In 1871 a new shop and post office was built for rent at the nearby crossroads and John McArthur was postmaster there; this was bought by Keith Campbell in 1895. In 1898 a new additional branch post office was opened in the eastern wing of the Pier House, receiving the mail from the various steamers which called at Carradale. The sub-postmistress was Miss Margaret Ritchie, who was succeeded by her nephew John as postmaster until the office closed in 1940. It was around this time that John (Jock) Paterson opened a post office at Ashbank in Airds. Subsequently this was moved to this building at the west crossroads, later Campbell's Stores, where it remained until the establishment in the 1960s of post offices in both Airds and Carradale West, the former of which was closed in 2017.

Originally run as an inn, Carradale Hotel became the first hotel in the village. The feu was granted to the McKinven family by the laird, Carrick Buchanan, in 1858 although the building wasn't erected until around 1870 when the number of tourists was increasing substantially. Its business was enhanced by the alcohol licence it obtained in 1890 and the residential accommodation was enlarged in the 1920s and again in 1960 when the original snug bar was converted and extended to become the Cruban Bar, so named after the maritime buoy off Port Righ Bay. The hotel's rooms and dining facilities have been upgraded and extended over the years and two squash courts were built in the 1970s, but these have since been demolished.

This petrol pump at the hotel was one of four in the village, including those at the pier, Campbells' Stores and the West Post Office. At the time of this photograph taken in the 1930s, it was still commonplace for petrol to be served to the motorist, here by Jim McDougall, the hotel owner. The nearest suppliers of petrol are now in Campbeltown and Clachan. The hotel also had a small shop which sold hardware, paint, fancy goods and ice cream and operated a small lending library, but all of these facilities closed many years ago when the public bar extension was built.

The hotel's alcohol licence lapsed in 1920, perhaps due to a local religious aversion to alcohol. A deputation of Carradale ladies at the time tried to stop the granting of a licence at Campbeltown Licensing Court and this succeeded with the support of the minister of the United Free Church at that time, the Rev. George S. MacLeod. The licence was restored in 1960. The McKinvens' daughter married Alistair MacDougall and their son, Jim, ran the hotel with his wife until the early 1990s, when his daughter and her husband John Martin, assisted by Stuart Irvine, kept up the family tradition, succeeded by the Adams family. The barmaid for many years was a lady from Deucheran, just north of the village, who it is said could clear the bar at closing time with just one look.

These four terraced cottages at Port Righ were built between 1881 and 1891, primarily for fishermen and their families: there were around twenty children living there. More houses of similar size were subsequently built above Port Righ bay. However, at the southern end of the road was built a large house called Dunvalanree, which operated as a boarding house from 1938, and as a very successful private hotel and up-market restaurant until 2017. On a corner of the narrow road leading down to Port Righ and across the fields from Airds was Port Righ well, the source of remarkably pure water. Known as the local wishing well, it used to be religiously maintained and was provided with a ladle and protected by a gate. It is currently being restored.

PORT RIGH BAY, CARRADALE

Port Righ is Gaelic for 'Port of the King' and tradition holds that Robert the Bruce, on his flight from Arran, landed on this shore. Port Righ bay was one of three havens around the village which provided safe shelter for fishing boats. Its gently sloping beach allowed boats to be brought onshore and between the wars rowing boats were available for hire.

The flat expanse of ground to the north-east of Port Righ bay was frequently used as a campsite during the summer months. Youngsters from Glasgow schools travelled by steamer to Campbeltown and were then transported by covered lorries to the village where they set up camp for two-week stretches. Bell tents were all that were available in those days and these tended to leak in the event of the (usual) rain. Fresh water was obtained from the spring beside the steps at the far end of the beach. Parents were encouraged to make the long journey there and back to visit their offspring over the middle weekend and treat them to local ice creams. Entertainment for the campers included searching for lost golf balls on the adjacent course.

A view of Port Righ with Dunvalanree in the middle foreground and Crimond to the middle right, the Tormhor houses in the top left and with Carradale Hotel, the bakery, and Airds in the top right. Born in Lossiemouth, Charlie Reppke (who appears in the photograph on page 54) set up a kippering business in Carradale and died in Campbeltown in 1957. To celebrate his adopted home he wrote 'Carradale song':

*I try to picture youthful scenes and live them o'er again. My thoughts take flight across the year and memory rends the veil. Once more I see revealed to me my native Carradale.*

*Carradale, Carradale, there's music in that name, a melody reminding me of youth and love and hame. I'm ever longing for the day I'll take the homeward trail, once more to gaze from Dippen's Braes on lovely Carradale.*

*In fancy my spirit takes the road up from the sea to Moineruach and Drumbuie and on the Kirnashie. And whether it be summer sun or winter's driving gale, there's beauty there beyond compare in lovely Carradale.*

*I've often trod the winding paths that skirt Kilbrannan shores, and waded through the heather bells that blossom on Tor Mhor. From Castle Rock at eventide I've watched the boats set sail, I've wished them back and safely back at morn to Carradale.*

The cottages on the Shore Road towards the bay of Port na Cuile were built in the 1870s and were sold to the existing tenants for around £150 each in 1947. Helendale, the large house at the end of the Shore Road, was built in 1902 by Lawrence McBride and later extended. This has been the home of Margaret McBride, who for many years delivered the mail on foot all around the village, with a permanent cheery smile. Port Na Cuile offered only very limited shelter from northerly or easterly winds. There was a small inlet leading onto the shore but it was unsafe for boats because the entrance was partially submerged by Sgeir a Bhoga, a low narrow rock which was covered at quarter tide.

Built in the early eighteenth century for Richard Campbell of Glen Carrdale, Carradale House was extended in 1844 by David Bryce, whose other work includes Fettes College in Edinburgh. The 'Big House', as it has long been known, and the estate were purchased by Dick and Naomi Mitchison in 1938, and they soon made it the centre of village life. By participating and encouraging fundraising events, the couple part-financed the building of the village hall in 1939/40 and gifted ownership of it to the village in 1978. One summer's night in 1969 a wing of the house went on fire, which was spotted from the bay by Archie Paterson in the *Harvest Queen,* and he alerted the Carradale and Campbeltown fire brigades. The wing was replaced and extended over subsequent years. Dick Mitchison was MP for Kettering and was given a peerage by Harold Wilson in 1964. He died in 1970 and his ashes were sprinkled on the bay from Archie's boat. Naomi became the Laird of Carradale and a generous hostess to villagers to whom the welcoming dram was freely offered. At New Year Carradale House was an open house, when villagers called to extend greetings and revel in a true ceilidh atmosphere. As she said, 'were the Big House to become part of the life of the surrounding countryside, its standards must not be too different: it must not overawe.' On her death in 1999, aged 101, the estate was purchased by Colin Burgess who operates the Carradale Bay Caravan Park. The estate included the cottage of the gamekeeper, Eddie Martindale, who in addition to working on the farm for the Mitchisons for 64 years, bred litters of Cairn terriers.

Copyright. CDL. 105

TORISDALE CASTLE, CARRADALE.

Raphael Tuck & Sons, Ltd. London.

Torrisdale Castle was built in 1815 for General Keith Macalister from a design by James Gillespie Graham, one of Scotland's most famous architects, and using Wigtownshire sandstone. By 1850 the estate population had grown to around 130 workers and tenants. Sir David Carrick Buchanan bought the lairdship of Torrisdale in 1858 and then rented the castle to Peter Hall in 1872, whose son William Macalister Hall bought the castle and estate in 1898 and extended the castle to the north and south in 1903 and 1908. The castle was listed category B in 1971. The Macalister Halls had a pew in their name in the local church and a resident of the village remembers his grandfather being the butler in the castle. In recent years the estate, still owned by the same family, has diversified into tourism, with rentable accommodation, a tannery and a gin distillery.

Torrisdale bridge was built in the eighteenth century and renovated in 1840. It was listed category C in 1980. It links the hamlet of Torrisdale with Bridgend in Carradale via the B842, inspiration for the Beatles' song 'The long and winding road'. To the south of Torrisdale lies Saddell Beach; this was used as the setting for the enormously successful promo film for the hit single 'Mull of Kintyre' by Paul McCartney and Wings, featuring the Campbeltown Pipe Band in full regalia.

Dippen bridge is on the southern approach to Carradale village (this view is looking north) and it was built in 1789 and listed category B in 1971. Its left junction in the foreground leads to the Church of Scotland parish church of Saddell and Skipness, which was originally built in 1753 and replaced in 1865. The church is listed category C. Beyond the church this road leads to Rhonadale, a farm whose owners have included the Forestry Commission wildlife ranger who had responsibility for the golden eagles in Carradale Glen. The right junction passes Semple's former dairy, established in 1938, and leads past an old cemetery to the small hamlet of Waterfoot, which was inhabited for many years by fishermen. In the right background of the view is the former United Free Church (see page 51) and in the centre of the view is the 1908 school and police house. The hill dominating the background is Creag an Daimh, which is around 200 metres in height.

STUDIO WATERFOOT, CARRADALE.

Waterfoot has inspired many artists with its quiet picturesque tranquility. During the nineteenth century it was home to members of the Glasgow Boys group of painters. One of Scotland's most famous artists, William McTaggart (1835-1910), was born in Kintyre and spent his schooldays in Campbeltown. He visited Machrihanish and Carradale frequently when in his prime and was particularly praised for his paintings of the sea on the west coast. He stayed in Ardcarrach, just above the pier in Carradale, and it was there that he completed his most impressive painting, 'The Storm', in the mid 1880s.

This was originally the North Lodge of the Carradale estate and between 1887 and 1891 it became the village's infant school with 12 to 15 children aged under seven attending. This was because the main school, with accommodation for 63 pupils and located at Auchnasavil further up the road in Carradale Glen, was regarded as too far from home for youngsters to travel on foot. Pupils were expected to bring a peat for the fire. The building was later used as a private house and after refurbishment by volunteers it recently became part of the tourist attraction Carradale Network Centre.

This is the original main school at Auchnasavil, also established in 1887. In 1888 the Inspector of Schools found that the register of pupils had 84 names, exceeding the nominal capacity by 21, even allowing for regular absentees. As a result, to replace both buildings a new primary school for children from five years old was built in 1890 south of the crossroads at Campbell's Stores, with separate entrances for boys and girls. The headmaster from 1898 was a Mr McInnes. Secondary education was conducted in Campbeltown's Grammar School. The primary closed in 1988 when it was replaced by a new building. The old one was then converted into private dwellings.

Carradale Football Club has been playing in local and Glasgow leagues since the 1920s. This photo is of the team at a match for the Sheriff McMaster Campbell Trophy, played at Kintyre Park in Campbeltown 1953. The team beat a strong Lochend United four goals to two and consisted of (*back row, left to right*) Colin Paterson, Donnely McMillan, Murray Shaw (one goal), Jack McIntosh, Donnie Kelly, Jock Paterson; (*front row*) John Ritchie, Colin Galbraith (two goals), Archie Paterson (one goal), a player whose name is unknown, and John McCorkindale.

The Free Church broke away from the established Church of Scotland in 1843 and the Free Church in Carradale was built in 1892. Following another merger this became the United Free Church in 1900. The United Free Church rejoined the Church of Scotland in 1929. The church is no longer in use and is empty while the manse to the right is now a restaurant. The building to the rear of the church was used as stables.

Operation Pied Piper – the evacuation of school children living in urban areas threatened by German bombers – began throughout the UK on 1 September 1939, two days before war was declared on Germany. The children were mainly transported by railways and, as can be seen here, sometimes by steamer. Teachers often accompanied their pupils. Each child carried a gas mask and was also expected to carry spare underclothes, night clothes, slippers, socks, toiletries and a warm coat, on which was pinned a label with their name, date of birth, school and destination. Children from the Glasgow area were evacuated to Carradale and remained with many local families until the end of the war, although some returned to the city in the following year when the danger of bombing appeared to have subsided. One couple on the Shore Road, who had no children of their own, kept in touch with their evacuees until they grew up and in turn became married themselves.

*Below*: A group of children gathered in front of the original golf course clubhouse. Carradale Golf Club was first established by the laird, Austin Mackenzie, in 1906. It consisted of nine holes, which included three holes located behind the house Dunvalanree in Port Righ. The Dunvalanree holes were lost when the current nine-hole course was created around the start of World War II. Medal tees were created in the early 1970s and the eighteen-hole course (players play the same nine holes off more distant medal tees) records are 65 for the ladies and 61 for the men, both by local members. The first clubhouse, shown here, had slatted flooring through which car keys and coins fell, often irretrievably! The clubhouse has been replaced twice over the years. The long-standing greenkeepers have been Duncan Fisher (1950s to 1970s) and Robert Strang (1990 to present).

Over the decades, bunkers have come and gone on the course and a dry stane dyke was eventually removed from in front of the seventh green. For many years the fifth green was lightning fast and sloping beneath the sixth tee until a new level green was built by Duncan Fisher into the bank above, which made the hole a much fairer test of ability. The fifteenth hole, named Pudding Bowl, is the signature hole of the course and precedes the next hole's medal tee, which is one of the toughest par 3's anywhere. Electric fences were erected around some of the greens to prevent damage caused by sheep and cattle roaming over the course, which is leased from a local farmer. July and August provided great fun for adults and children, with a variety of competitions organized by a small committee of annual visitors. In the days when the photograph above was taken, after prizes were awarded the children would all proceed along to Lochpark Café for ice cream.

Soon after the start of World War II observation posts were built overlooking Kilbrannan Sound to monitor naval movements by the enemy. This one was situated at the highest point on Carradale golf course, and was manned by men deemed too old for active service but too young to join the Home Guard. The Royal Observer Corps Team was (*back row, left to right*) Tom Paterson, John Paterson, Berty MacAlister, Donald MacLaren, Hugh McGriggart, Donald McIntosh and Charley Reppke; (*front row*) Angus Buchanan, Alex McMillan, Charles McDougal, unnamed, and Donald Morrison. An anti-submarine boom was placed at the entrance to Campbeltown Loch, which was seen as a strategic safe harbour. Two Royal Navy planes crashed in the area in 1944 with the loss of six lives; the second had been engaged in practice bombing at a range at Skipness.

Five miles north of Carradale lies the hamlet of Grogport. At the 1861 census there was a population of forty living in seven houses. There is a converted church that stands alongside a sandy beach named Garrachroit Bay, into which runs Grogport Burn. A small shop was operated early in the twentieth century by Colin Campbell, selling groceries and sweets. At the north end of the beach is the former Sunadale Inn, a one-time public house, to which agricultural workers and fishermen from Carradale frequently trekked on Sundays. These thirsty men enjoyed ale and whisky but these were social outings and incidences of drunkenness were rare. At the time, there was no similar establishment in Carradale until 1960, when the hotel successfully renewed its full licence. The Sunadale Inn remained in business until being converted into a private dwelling around 1950.

Stepping Stones, Waterfoot, Carradale.

A sign from the Big Bay – also known as the 'Silver Sands' – leads to these long-standing stepping stones, which cross the Carra Water some distance below a former bridge of which there is now only ruins. They only offer a safe crossing at low water. Further downstream there used to be a jetty for unloading boats. In past years fishermen living in Waterfoot would cross the river at this point, then walk to the east end of Carradale estate and pass through the Fisherman's Gate, a metal gate on the border of the estate below Nicholson's Brae on the main road. They would then walk over a mile to the harbour, where their boats were moored.

There was never much call for a police presence in Carradale and the police house was eventually closed in 2018 in favour of the station at Campbeltown. John MacBrayne MM, seen here, served as the local policeman from 1939 to 1953. Later, Sandy McDougall was renowned for arriving at the Cruban public bar shortly before closing time to verify that no improper activities were taking place.